Iowa Bingo Book

COMPLETE BINGO GAME IN A BOOK

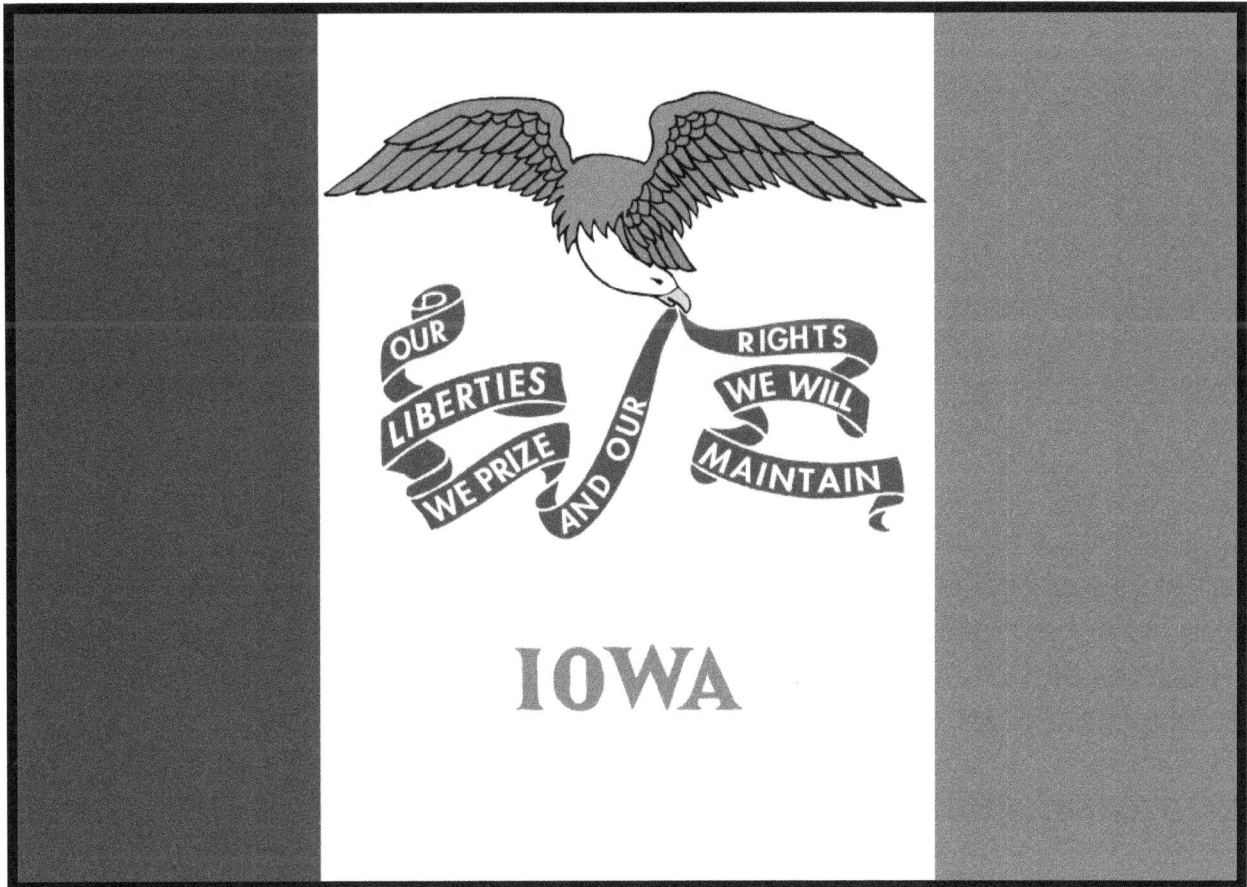

IOWA

Written By Rebecca Stark

ISBN 978-0-87386-508-1

Educational Books 'n' Bingo

Printed in the U.S.A.

DIRECTIONS

INCLUDED:

List of Terms

Templates for Additional Terms and Clues

2 Clues per Term

30 Unique Bingo Cards

Markers

1. **Either cut apart the book or make copies of ALL the sheets. You might want to make an extra copy of the clue sheets to use for introduction and review. Keep the sheets in an envelope for easy reuse.**

2. Cut apart the call cards with terms and clues.

3. Pass out one bingo card per student. There are enough for a class of 30.

4. Pass out markers. You may cut apart the markers included in this book or use any other small items of your choice.

5. Decide whether or not you will require the entire card to be filled. Requiring the entire card to be filled provides a better review. However, if you have a short time to fill, you may prefer to have them do the just the border or some other format. Tell the class before you begin what is required.

6. There are 50 terms. Read the list before you begin. If there are any terms that have not been covered in class, you may want to read to the students the term and clues before you begin.

7. There is a blank space in the middle of each card. You can instruct the students to use it as a free space or you can write in answers to cover terms not included. Of course, in this case you would create your own clues. (Templates provided.)

8. Shuffle the cards and place them in a pile. Two or three clues are provided for each term. If you plan to play the game with the same group more than once, you might want to choose a different clue for each game. If not, you may choose to use more than one clue.

9. Be sure to keep the cards you have used for the present game in a separate pile. When a student calls, "Bingo," he or she will have to verify that the correct answers are on his or her card AND that the markers were placed in response to the proper questions. Pull out the cards that are on the student's card keeping them in the order they were used in the game. Read each clue as it was given and ask the student to identify the correct answer from his or her card.

10. If the student has the correct answers on the card AND has shown that they were marked in response to the *correct questions,* then that student is the winner and the game is over. If the student does not have the correct answers on the card OR he or she marked the answers in response to *the wrong questions,* then the game continues until there is a proper winner.

11. If you want to play again, reshuffle the cards and begin again.

Have fun!

TERMS INCLUDED

Black Hawk

Border(s)

Cedar Rapids

Climate

William Frederick Cody

Corn

Council Bluffs

County (-ies)

Crop(s)

Des Moines

Dissected Till Plains

Drift

Driftless Area

Dubuque

Eastern Goldfinch

Effigy Mounds

Executive Branch

Flag

Geode(s)

Hawkeye State

Herbert Clark Hoover

Highest Point

Industry (-ies)

Iowa City

Iowa Territory

Ioway

Judicial Branch

Lake Red Rock

Legislative Branch

Lewis and Clark

Livestock

Louisiana Purchase

Marquette and Jolliet

Mississippi River

Missouri River

Motto

Native American

Oak

Prairie

Railroads

Rivers

Seal

Song

State Fair

Till

Union

University of Iowa

Wild Prairie Rose

Grant Wood

Young Drift Plains

Additional Terms

Choose as many additional terms as you would like and write them in the squares. Repeat each as desired.
Cut out the squares and randomly distribute them to the class.
Instruct the students to place their square on the center space of their card.

Iowa Bingo

Clues for Additional Terms

Write three clues for each of your additional terms.

_____ 1. 2. 3.	_____ 1. 2. 3.
_____ 1. 2. 3.	_____ 1. 2. 3.
_____ 1. 2. 3.	_____ 1. 2. 3.

Iowa Bingo

IOWA IOWA IOWA IOWA IOWA

IOWA IOWA IOWA IOWA IOWA

IOWA IOWA IOWA IOWA IOWA

IOWA IOWA IOWA IOWA IOWA

IOWA IOWA IOWA IOWA IOWA

IOWA IOWA IOWA IOWA IOWA

IOWA IOWA IOWA IOWA IOWA

Black Hawk 1. ___ was a Sauk warrior. During the War of 1812, he fought on the side of the British. He led a band of Sauk during the brief conflict named for him. 2. After the ___ War, the Sauk had to cede the land west of the Mississippi River to the U.S., opening the land to white settlement.	**Border(s)** 1. These states ___ Iowa: Minnesota, Missouri, Wisconsin, Illinois, South Dakota and Nebraska. 2. Iowa's east and west ___ are formed by rivers: the Mississippi on the east and the Missouri on the west.
Cedar Rapids 1. Located on the Cedar River, ___ is the second largest city in Iowa. 2. ___ is nicknamed the "City of Five Seasons." A sculpture named the "Tree of Five Seasons" is in the downtown area of the city.	**Climate** 1. Iowa has a humid continental ___. 2. Like other Midwestern states, the ___ of Iowa is affected by the Great Lakes and the region's location in the middle of the continent.
William Frederick Cody 1. ___ was born in Scott County in 1846. His nickname was "Buffalo Bill." 2. ___ was a soldier, frontiersman, and showman.	**Corn** 1. The ___ Belt is a region of the Midwest where corn has replaced the native tall grasses as the dominant crop. 2. The United States produces 40% of the world's supply of ___. Iowa leads the states in the production of this crop.
Council Bluffs 1. When ___ was designated as the eastern terminus for the Union Pacific, it became a major railroad center. 2. This city on the east bank of the Missouri River ___ was the historic starting point of the Mormon Trail.	**County (-ies)** 1. There are 99 ___ in Iowa. 2. Polk ___ is the most densely populated ___. Des Moines, the state capital and largest city, is in Polk ___.
Crop(s) 1. Corn and soybeans are major cash ___ in Iowa. Iowa leads the states in the production of corn. 2. In addition to corn and soybeans, major field ___ include oats and hay, red clover, flaxseed, rye and wheat. Iowa Bingo	**Des Moines** 1. ___ is the capital and most populous city in Iowa. 2. ___ is the site of the annual Iowa State Fair.

Dissected Till Plains	**Drift**
1. The region known as the ___ stretches across the southern part of Iowa. It extends north along the Missouri and Big Sioux rivers. 2. The drift that was deposited long ago by glaciers in the region known as the ___ is called till. Rivers and streams dissected, or cut into, the terrain forming low, rolling hills and ridges.	1. Earth and rocks that have been transported by moving ice is called glacial ___. 2. The Young ___ Plains are mostly flat, fertile lands. This land had been covered by ___ left by glaciers during the ice age.
Driftless Area	**Dubuque**
1. The region called the ___ is in northeastern Iowa. It is called this because drift that was deposited here was blown or washed away. 2. The land region called the ___ is not as flat as the Young Drift Plains. This region has many pine-forested hills.	1. ___ is at the junction of three states: Iowa, Illinois, and Wisconsin. It was named after a pioneer from Quebec, the first permanent settler in the area. 2. The Fourth Street Elevator, also known as the Fenelon Place Elevator, is a funicular railway located in ___.
Eastern Goldfinch	**Effigy Mounds**
1. The ___ is the state bird. The male has a bright yellow body. 2. Also called the wild canary, the ___ is found throughout Iowa. It often stays through the winter months.	1. ___ National Monument preserves 200 prehistoric American Indian mound sites built along the Mississippi River between 450 BC and 1300 CE. 2. More than 200 Native American mounds can be seen at ___ National Monument in the Upper Mississippi River Valley.
Executive Branch	**Flag**
1. The ___ comprises the governor, the lieutenant governor, the secretary of state, the auditor of state, the treasurer of state, the secretary of agriculture, and the attorney general. 2. The governor is head of the ___. The present-day governor is [fill in].	1. There are 3 vertical stripes on the state ___: blue, white and red. 2. In the center of the ___'s broad white stripe is an eagle; it carries streamers inscribed with the state's motto.
Geode(s)	**Hawkeye State**
1. The ___ is the state rock. Many rare and beautiful ___ can found in the state. 2. ___ have a hard outer shell; when cut, there is a core of sparkling mineral crystals.	1. Iowa is known as the ___. Another nickname is the "Corn State." 2. Some say this nickname was a tribute to Chief Black Hawk. Others say it was named after a character in *The Last of the Mohicans,* by James Fenimore Cooper.

Iowa Bingo

Herbert Clark Hoover 1. This Iowan was the 31st President of the United States. He was originally a mining engineer. 2. This President of the United States was born in West Branch, Iowa. He was secretary of commerce before becoming President.	**Highest Point** 1. The ___ in the state was officially named Hawkeye Point in 1998. 2. The ___ in Iowa is near Sibley in Osceola County. It is 1,670 feet in height.
Industry (-ies) 1. Food processing is the largest manufacturing ___ in Iowa. 2. Although agriculture is the mainstay of the state's economy, the manufacture of farm machinery and construction equipment are also important ___.	**Iowa City** 1. ___ was the second capital of Iowa Territory and the first capital of the state of Iowa. 2. The University of Iowa is in ___.
Iowa Territory 1. Iowa was part of Wisconsin Territory from 1836 to 1838, when Congress created ___. 2. Burlington was the capital of ___ until Iowa City was made its official capital in 1841.	**Ioway** 1. The ___, or Iowa, are Native American Siouan people. 2. The name Iowa comes from the ___ people, one of the Native American tribes that occupied the region at the time of European exploration.
Judicial Branch 1. The ___ interprets what our laws mean and makes decisions about the laws and those who break them. 2. The ___ is made up of several courts, the highest of which is the state Supreme Court.	**Lake Red Rock** 1. ___ was formed by the creation of Red Rock Dam on the Des Moines River. 2. ___ is the largest lake in Iowa; it was created by the United States Army Corps of Engineers as part of a flood-control project.
Legislative Branch 1. The General Assembly is the ___ of the state government. It is composed of the Iowa Senate and the Iowa House of Representatives. 2. The ___ makes the laws. Iowa Bingo	**Lewis and Clark** 1. The purpose of the ___Expedition, also known as the Corps of Discovery Expedition, was to explore the vast unknown territory west of the Mississippi River. 2. On August 10, 1804, the Corps of Discovery arrived at the area where the ___ State Park now lies.

Livestock
1. Hogs are Iowa's leading source of ___ income. More hogs are raised in Iowa than in any other state.
2. After hogs, beef cattle are the most important ___ product. Milk, chickens and eggs are also important.

Louisiana Purchase
1. Present-day Iowa came to the United States as part of the ___. Before that the area was part of New France.
2. The ___ of 1803 doubled the size of the United States and opened up the continent to its westward expansion.

Marquette and Jolliet
1. ___ were the first Europeans to follow the course of the Mississippi River.
2. The ___ expedition were the first Europeans to visit Iowa.

Mississippi River
1. The ___ is the chief river of the largest river system in North America.
2. The ___ forms the entire eastern border of Iowa. Dubuque, Keokuk, Davenport, and Clinton are on the ___.

Missouri River
1. The ___ is the longest river in North America. It is a tributary of the Mississippi River.
2. The ___ forms the entire western border of Iowa. Carter Lake, Council Bluffs, and Sioux City are on the ___.

Motto
1. The state ___ is "Our liberties we prize and our rights we will maintain."
2. The state ___ is on the state flag and the Great Seal.

Native American
1. There were many ___ tribes in Iowa at the time of European exploration.
2. Many ___ were forced to leave their homelands in the 1800s for reservations in Kansas, Nebraska, and Oklahoma.

Oak
1. The ___ is the state tree.
2. The ___ is abundant in the state. It is an important commercial timber crop.

Prairie
1. A ___ is an extensive area of flat or rolling, mostly treeless grassland.
2. Iowa is sometimes called the "Land of the Rolling ___."

Railroads
1. The building of ___ in the second half of the 19th century brought major economic changes to Iowa.
2. One reason ___ were important was that they provided year-round transportation for farmers.

Iowa Bingo

Rivers

1. The Cedar, Des Moines, Iowa, Mississippi, and Missouri are important ___ of Iowa.
2. Iowa is the only state whose east and west borders are formed entirely by ___.

Seal

1. In the middle of the Great ___ is a soldier in a field of wheat.
2. Above the soldier on the Great ___ is an eagle; in its beak is a scroll with the state's motto.

Song

1. The state ___ is entitled "Song of Iowa."
2. The first line of the state ___ is "You asked what land I love the best, Iowa, tis Iowa…"

State Fair

1. The Iowa ___ is one of the oldest and largest agricultural and industrial expositions in the country.
2. The 2011 Iowa ___ marked the 100th anniversary of the butter cow sculpture.

Till

1. ___ is unsorted drift that has been deposited directly by glacial ice.
2. ___ is glacial drift consisting of an unsorted mixture of clay, sand, gravel, and boulders.

Union

1. The southeastern portion of Iowa Territory was admitted to the ___ as the state of Iowa   on December 28, 1846.
2. No Civil War battle was fought on Iowa soil, but many Iowans volunteered to fight for the ___.

University of Iowa

1. The ___ was the first public university in the country to admit women and men on an equal basis.
2. This institution of higher learning was founded shortly after Iowa became a state. It is   in Iowa City.

Wild Prairie Rose

1. The ___ is the state flower.
2. The ___ grows naturally throughout North America. Its petals come in varying shades of pink. Its stamens are yellow.

Grant Wood

1. This American painter was born in Iowa in 1891. The design on the state quarter is based on one of his paintings; it is named "Arbor Day."
2. ___ is known for his paintings depicting the rural American Midwest. "American Gothic" is his most famous painting.

Young Drift Plains

1. The ___ covers most of northern and central Iowa. The land in this region is mostly flat and fertile.
2. The drift left in the ___ by glaciers during the ice age resulted in some of the most fertile topsoil in the world.

Iowa Bingo

Iowa Bingo

Oak	Black Hawk	Cedar Rapids	Geode(s)	William Frederick Cody
Executive Branch	Border(s)	Wild Prairie Rose	Lewis and Clark	Rivers
University of Iowa	Legislative Branch		Missouri River	Grant Wood
Union	Railroads	Till	Lake Red Rock	Louisiana Purchase
Mississippi River	Highest Point	Dubuque	Song	Iowa Territory

Iowa Bingo: Card No. 1

Iowa Bingo

Union	University of Iowa	Iowa City	Prairie	Judicial Branch
Louisiana Purchase	Eastern Goldfinch	County (-ies)	Railroads	Marquette and Jolliet
Des Moines	Highest Point		Industry (-ies)	Till
Motto	Native American	Legislative Branch	Young Drift Plains	William Frederick Cody
Rivers	Wild Prairie Rose	Dubuque	Executive Branch	Song

Iowa Bingo

Highest Point	Till	Eastern Goldfinch	Lake Red Rock	University of Iowa
Louisiana Purchase	Border(s)	Crop(s)	Black Hawk	Herbert Clark Hoover
Railroads	Wild Prairie Rose		Marquette and Jolliet	Climate
Legislative Branch	Des Moines	Mississippi River	Motto	Iowa City
Song	Dissected Till Plains	Dubuque	Young Drift Plains	Judicial Branch

Iowa Bingo: Card No. 3

Iowa Bingo

Legislative Branch	Marquette and Jolliet	Cedar Rapids	Dissected Till Plains	Judicial Branch
Livestock	Council Bluffs	Black Hawk	Prairie	University of Iowa
Missouri River	Motto		Iowa Territory	Geode(s)
Till	Border(s)	Wild Prairie Rose	Dubuque	County (-ies)
Drift	Rivers	Corn	Song	Grant Wood

Iowa Bingo: Card No. 4

© Barbara M. Peller

Iowa Bingo

Rivers	William Frederick Cody	Railroads	County (-ies)	Dissected Till Plains
Livestock	Till	Crop(s)	Industry (-ies)	Border(s)
Cedar Rapids	Grant Wood		Lewis and Clark	Hawkeye State
Iowa Territory	Judicial Branch	Oak	Young Drift Plains	Driftless Area
Eastern Goldfinch	Dubuque	University of Iowa	Legislative Branch	Missouri River

© Barbara M. Peller

Iowa Bingo

Climate	Marquette and Jolliet	Iowa City	Judicial Branch	Grant Wood
Lake Red Rock	Railroads	Driftless Area	Black Hawk	University of Iowa
Prairie	Drift		Council Bluffs	Industry (-ies)
Dubuque	Mississippi River	Young Drift Plains	Corn	Cedar Rapids
Louisiana Purchase	County (-ies)	Oak	Missouri River	Effigy Mounds

Iowa Bingo

Oak	Marquette and Jolliet	Hawkeye State	Till	Eastern Goldfinch
Louisiana Purchase	Judicial Branch	Highest Point	Border(s)	Livestock
Grant Wood	Geode(s)		Industry (-ies)	Council Bluffs
Legislative Branch	Motto	Crop(s)	Union	Des Moines
Dubuque	Dissected Till Plains	Young Drift Plains	Corn	Climate

Iowa Bingo: Card No. 7

Iowa Bingo

Missouri River	Marquette and Jolliet	Flag	Lake Red Rock	Council Bluffs
Livestock	Cedar Rapids	Prairie	Grant Wood	County (-ies)
Effigy Mounds	Dissected Till Plains		Judicial Branch	William Frederick Cody
Song	Legislative Branch	Union	Drift	Motto
Wild Prairie Rose	Dubuque	Corn	Railroads	Louisiana Purchase

Iowa Bingo: Card No. 8

Iowa Bingo

Industry (-ies)	Eastern Goldfinch	Highest Point	Effigy Mounds	Dissected Till Plains
Drift	Judicial Branch	Missouri River	Railroads	Marquette and Jolliet
Herbert Clark Hoover	Oak		Border(s)	Flag
Driftless Area	William Frederick Cody	Mississippi River	Lewis and Clark	Hawkeye State
Motto	Young Drift Plains	Crop(s)	Union	Iowa Territory

Iowa Bingo: Card No. 9

Iowa Bingo

Union	Lake Red Rock	Council Bluffs	Prairie	Effigy Mounds
Grant Wood	County (-ies)	Black Hawk	Border(s)	Judicial Branch
Dissected Till Plains	Marquette and Jolliet		Geode(s)	Des Moines
Mississippi River	Iowa Territory	Driftless Area	Young Drift Plains	Herbert Clark Hoover
Crop(s)	Louisiana Purchase	Iowa City	Rivers	Missouri River

Iowa Bingo: Card No. 10

Iowa
Bingo

Climate	Marquette and Jolliet	Railroads	Driftless Area	Louisiana Purchase
Flag	Herbert Clark Hoover	Lewis and Clark	Industry (-ies)	Black Hawk
Livestock	Judicial Branch		Iowa City	Highest Point
Crop(s)	University of Iowa	Young Drift Plains	Dissected Till Plains	Union
Drift	Dubuque	Oak	Corn	Eastern Goldfinch

Iowa Bingo

Eastern Goldfinch	William Frederick Cody	Herbert Clark Hoover	Lake Red Rock	Industry (-ies)
Highest Point	Louisiana Purchase	Cedar Rapids	Corn	Border(s)
Oak	Hawkeye State		Grant Wood	Prairie
Dubuque	Motto	Judicial Branch	Union	Livestock
Marquette and Jolliet	Flag	Dissected Till Plains	Drift	County (-ies)

Iowa Bingo

Driftless Area	William Frederick Cody	Climate	Herbert Clark Hoover	Grant Wood
Cedar Rapids	Flag	Judicial Branch	Industry (-ies)	Des Moines
Lake Red Rock	County (-ies)		Highest Point	Hawkeye State
Missouri River	Young Drift Plains	Council Bluffs	Dissected Till Plains	Union
Dubuque	Iowa Territory	Corn	Oak	Lewis and Clark

Iowa
Bingo

Iowa Bingo

Executive Branch	Judicial Branch	Railroads	Industry (-ies)	Drift
County (-ies)	Oak	Herbert Clark Hoover	Border(s)	Marquette and Jolliet
Driftless Area	Geode(s)		Iowa City	Crop(s)
Iowa Territory	Young Drift Plains	Dissected Till Plains	Council Bluffs	Climate
Dubuque	Prairie	Des Moines	Louisiana Purchase	Missouri River

Iowa Bingo: Card No. 14

Iowa Bingo

Lewis and Clark	Industry (-ies)	Railroads	Eastern Goldfinch	Lake Red Rock
Climate	Iowa City	Black Hawk	Cedar Rapids	Drift
Grant Wood	Oak		University of Iowa	Marquette and Jolliet
Dubuque	Herbert Clark Hoover	Flag	Young Drift Plains	Driftless Area
Louisiana Purchase	Motto	Corn	Effigy Mounds	Highest Point

Iowa Bingo: Card No. 15

Iowa Bingo

Council Bluffs	Herbert Clark Hoover	Flag	Effigy Mounds	Native American
Prairie	Des Moines	Hawkeye State	Livestock	Geode(s)
Driftless Area	William Frederick Cody		Grant Wood	Highest Point
Legislative Branch	County (-ies)	Dubuque	Lewis and Clark	Union
Drift	State Fair	Corn	Motto	Marquette and Jolliet

Iowa Bingo

Crop(s)	Seal	Ioway	Herbert Clark Hoover	Executive Branch
Lewis and Clark	Drift	Young Drift Plains	Geode(s)	Hawkeye State
Industry (-ies)	Missouri River		State Fair	Flag
Iowa Territory	Louisiana Purchase	Union	Railroads	Des Moines
Mississippi River	Driftless Area	Eastern Goldfinch	Lake Red Rock	William Frederick Cody

Iowa Bingo: Card No. 17

Iowa Bingo

Effigy Mounds	Dissected Till Plains	County (-ies)	Driftless Area	Prairie
Marquette and Jolliet	Crop(s)	Mississippi River	Grant Wood	Drift
Industry (-ies)	Des Moines		Ioway	Cedar Rapids
William Frederick Cody	Black Hawk	Young Drift Plains	Union	Iowa City
State Fair	Herbert Clark Hoover	Railroads	Seal	Climate

Iowa Bingo

Grant Wood	Climate	Herbert Clark Hoover	Flag	Union
Lewis and Clark	Lake Red Rock	Marquette and Jolliet	Eastern Goldfinch	Geode(s)
Seal	Dissected Till Plains		Border(s)	University of Iowa
Iowa City	State Fair	Mississippi River	Motto	Ioway
Cedar Rapids	Native American	Louisiana Purchase	Missouri River	Corn

Iowa Bingo: Card No. 19

Iowa Bingo

Executive Branch	Seal	Lake Red Rock	Herbert Clark Hoover	Corn
County (-ies)	Highest Point	Livestock	Mississippi River	Prairie
William Frederick Cody	Hawkeye State		Legislative Branch	Black Hawk
Rivers	Wild Prairie Rose	Song	Motto	State Fair
Till	Missouri River	Native American	Union	Ioway

Iowa Bingo

Lewis and Clark	Climate	Livestock	Herbert Clark Hoover	Rivers
William Frederick Cody	Ioway	Council Bluffs	Flag	Oak
Des Moines	Louisiana Purchase		Seal	Railroads
Mississippi River	Eastern Goldfinch	State Fair	Iowa Territory	Missouri River
Legislative Branch	Native American	Corn	Crop(s)	Motto

Iowa Bingo: Card No. 21

Iowa Bingo

Effigy Mounds	Iowa City	Ioway	Cedar Rapids	Driftless Area
Prairie	Lake Red Rock	University of Iowa	Flag	Border(s)
County (-ies)	Geode(s)		Oak	Hawkeye State
State Fair	Iowa Territory	Motto	Black Hawk	Livestock
Native American	Crop(s)	Seal	Des Moines	Legislative Branch

Iowa Bingo

Council Bluffs	Seal	Eastern Goldfinch	Cedar Rapids	Corn
Climate	Executive Branch	Louisiana Purchase	Lewis and Clark	Black Hawk
Iowa City	Driftless Area		Song	Oak
Des Moines	Native American	State Fair	Crop(s)	Motto
Rivers	Wild Prairie Rose	Missouri River	Mississippi River	Ioway

Iowa Bingo

Council Bluffs	Missouri River	Executive Branch	Seal	Flag
Ioway	Corn	Livestock	Prairie	Oak
Hawkeye State	Effigy Mounds		Driftless Area	Des Moines
Rivers	Song	State Fair	Crop(s)	William Frederick Cody
Till	Legislative Branch	Native American	Lake Red Rock	Wild Prairie Rose

Iowa Bingo

Legislative Branch	Livestock	Seal	Railroads	Ioway
Black Hawk	William Frederick Cody	Lewis and Clark	Council Bluffs	Border(s)
Iowa Territory	Flag		Song	State Fair
University of Iowa	Rivers	Wild Prairie Rose	Native American	Geode(s)
Corn	Executive Branch	County (-ies)	Drift	Till

Iowa Bingo: Card No. 25

© Barbara M. Peller

Iowa Bingo

Ioway	Seal	Iowa City	Prairie	Effigy Mounds
Mississippi River	Lake Red Rock	Flag	Executive Branch	Council Bluffs
Iowa Territory	Song		Geode(s)	Legislative Branch
Crop(s)	Cedar Rapids	Rivers	Native American	State Fair
Hawkeye State	Drift	Railroads	Wild Prairie Rose	Till

Iowa Bingo

Iowa City	County (-ies)	Seal	Executive Branch	Highest Point
Rivers	Song	Lewis and Clark	State Fair	Border(s)
Young Drift Plains	Wild Prairie Rose		Native American	Legislative Branch
Effigy Mounds	Climate	Livestock	Till	Black Hawk
Drift	Geode(s)	Ioway	University of Iowa	Hawkeye State

Iowa Bingo: Card No. 27

Iowa Bingo

Iowa City	Executive Branch	University of Iowa	Seal	Council Bluffs
Highest Point	Ioway	Song	Prairie	Geode(s)
Wild Prairie Rose	Des Moines		Hawkeye State	Mississippi River
Union	Effigy Mounds	Louisiana Purchase	Native American	State Fair
Cedar Rapids	Industry (-ies)	Drift	Till	Rivers

Iowa Bingo: Card No. 28

Iowa Bingo

Ioway	Executive Branch	Effigy Mounds	Lewis and Clark	Industry (-ies)
Motto	Mississippi River	Livestock	Hawkeye State	University of Iowa
Iowa Territory	Song		Border(s)	Seal
Highest Point	Rivers	Judicial Branch	Native American	State Fair
Council Bluffs	Flag	Till	Climate	Wild Prairie Rose

Iowa Bingo: Card No. 29

Iowa Bingo

Dissected Till Plains	Seal	Prairie	Industry (-ies)	State Fair
Black Hawk	Executive Branch	Iowa City	Geode(s)	Border(s)
Iowa Territory	Driftless Area		Hawkeye State	Livestock
Till	Climate	Cedar Rapids	Native American	Song
Rivers	Grant Wood	Wild Prairie Rose	Ioway	University of Iowa

Iowa Bingo: Card No. 30

www.ingramcontent.com/pod-product-compliance
Lightning Source LLC
LaVergne TN
LVHW061337060426
835511LV00014B/1980

9 780873 865081